Early Hunting Tools

An Introduction to Flintknapping

By Matt Gravelle

D1732981

Contents

Introduction

Tools with sharp edges were needed to hunt and butcher animals in the early days of hunting and gathering. At first, spears and knives were made of wood, bone, and horn. But man eventually saw that rocks with glass-like properties could break in a controlled manner, producing very sharp blades and projectile points. This observation led to the art of flintknapping.

Flintknapping is the process of chipping or breaking rocks into sharp-edged tools. Pieces or flakes of stone are chipped away, leaving what is called a flaked tool.

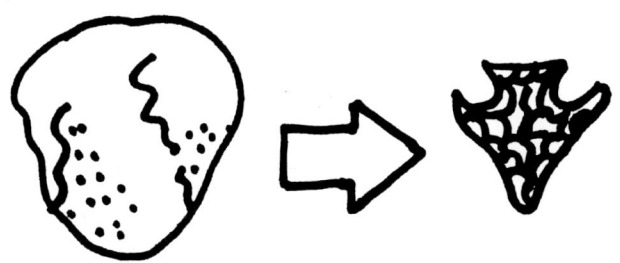

The ability to flintknap greatly helped the hunters and gatherers. However, this technology depended on an earlier and simpler tool called the hammerstone.

Tool Discovery

Plain rocks were discovered as useful tools 2.5 million years ago.

Early inhabitants used hammerstones to crush nuts and seeds, and break animal bones for the marrow.

The hammerstone led to a new discovery. It was noticed that certain rocks broke into very sharp pieces when struck by a hammerstone. This may have been discovered in a moment of frustration, curiosity, or downright luck.

The earliest flaked tool is known by researchers as the Oldowan pebble tool. Having one crudely flaked edge, this simple scraper and chopper developed in East Africa between 1.5 and 2.5 million years ago.

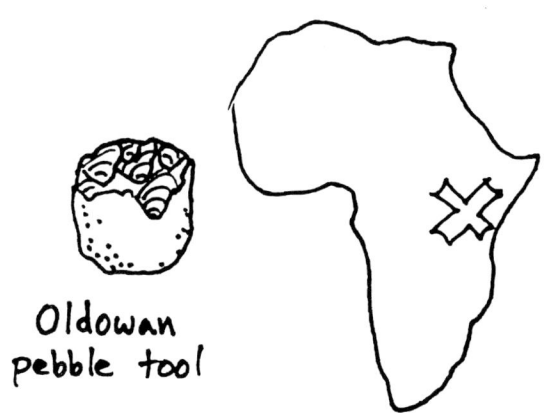

Oldowan
pebble tool

Eventually, a better tool developed, known as the Acheulean hand ax. It was flaked on all sides and provided a much sharper edge for cutting and scraping. The hand ax shows us that early hunters had a good understanding of the methods and materials involved in flintknapping.

Acheulean
hand ax

Material

Not every kind of rock will make a tool. In order for a rock to flake correctly, it must have glass-like or <u>vitreous</u> properties.

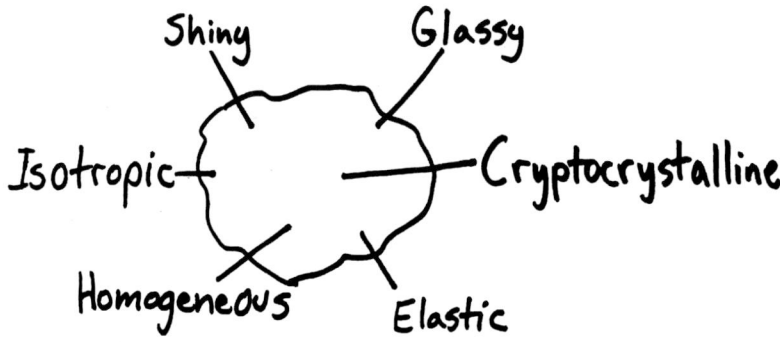

Good flintknapping stone is shiny and glassy. It has a <u>cryptocrystalline</u>, or very small crystal structure which is <u>isotropic</u>--the same in all directions. The stone is <u>elastic</u>, being able to hold its shape after being struck. And finally, the composition is <u>homogeneous</u>, or very pure. But perfect stone is difficult to find, and even the best natural material will have some impurities.

Types of stone commonly used by early man to make sharp tools include obsidian, flint, chert, rhyolite, chalcedony, and basalt. The late Don Crabtree, who pioneered modern flintknapping research, was famous for testing the flakability of many types of stone.

NAME ANY ROCK AND I'LL TELL YOU IF IT FLAKES.

Usually, sedimentary rocks like shale and sandstone are not good for flaking. However, igneous or volcanic rocks are good. Basalt is the most common igneous rock found, but obsidian is preferred for the sharp edge it produces.

metal
razor   obsidian

With no crystal structure, obsidian is basically a natural glass.

Cone Principle

The way a glassy rock breaks is described as the <u>cone principle</u>. As force is applied, energy spreads evenly, producing a cone-shaped or conchoidal fracture.

When force is applied to an edge, energy cannot travel outside the material. Instead, it reflects back into the stone. This is called <u>spalling</u>.

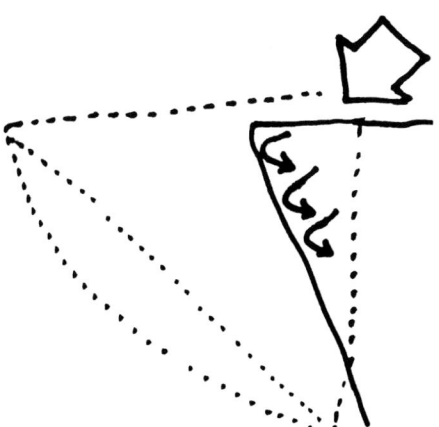

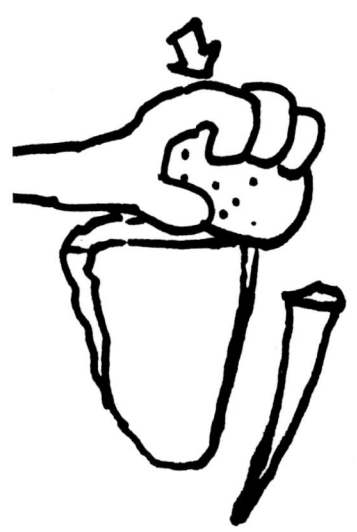

Instead of a circular cone, a longer half-cone is formed. The piece that breaks off is the <u>flake</u>.

The fracture side of the flake is called the <u>ventral</u> side, while the exterior side is called the <u>dorsal</u> side. The slight bulge of the ventral side is called the <u>positive bulb of force</u>.

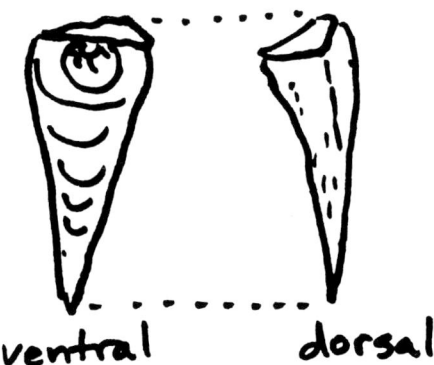

ventral   dorsal

The <u>negative bulb of force</u> refers to the cup-shaped scar left on the main piece of stone after a flake is removed. The horizontal ripples are called <u>compression rings</u>.

If you look in your cupboard and find chipped dishes and cups, the chipped scars may be conchoidal fractures. Early man worked hard at being able to produce this type of break.

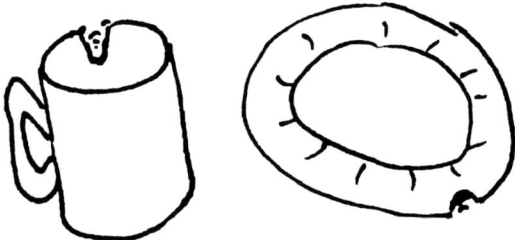

Several factors must be considered when
striking a flake. First, energy follows ridges.
Direct force over the top of a vertical ridge
should form a flake down the center of it.

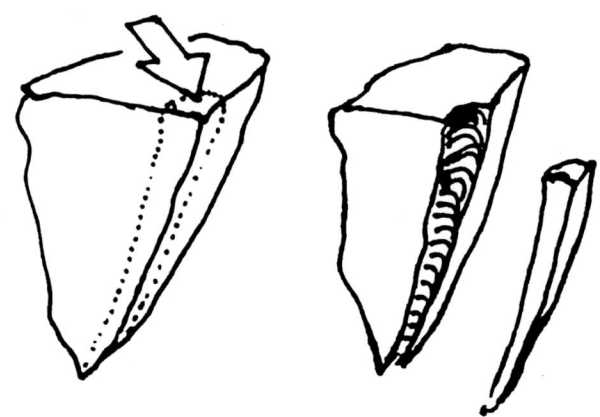

The angle of applied force relative to the surface or <u>platform</u> being struck must be less than 90°.

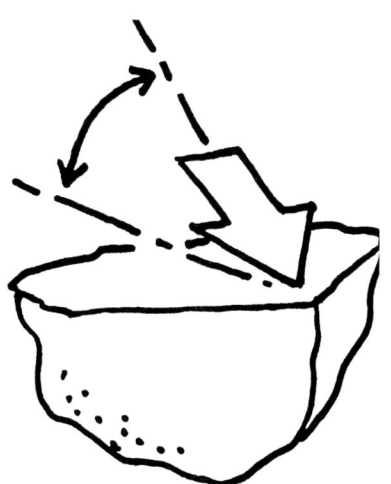

And finally, the angle of the stone's edge must also be less than 90°.

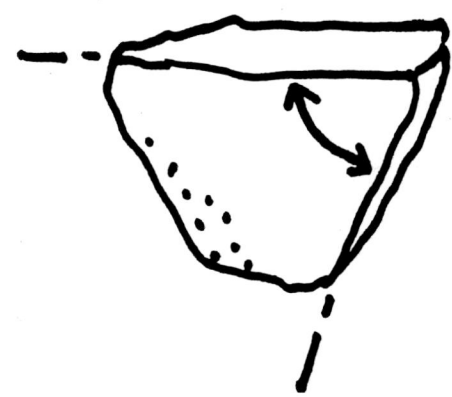

A toolmaker tries to imagine exactly how a stone will break before striking it.

The <u>proximal</u> end of a flake is the end that was struck, and the <u>distal</u> end is the bottom that is usually feathered into a sharp cutting edge. The side edges are called <u>margins</u>.

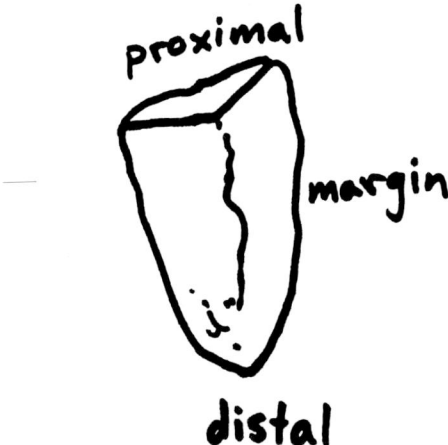

While a <u>feather fracture</u> is the ideal flake generated by the cone principle, <u>step fractures</u> and <u>hinge fractures</u> can occur because of wrong angles, wrong amounts of force, or impurities in the stone.

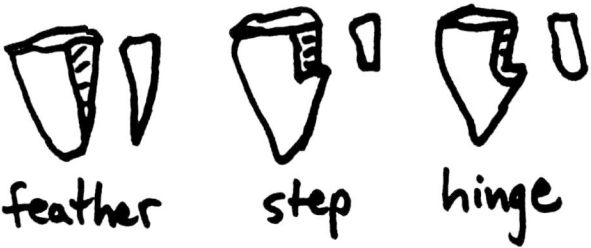

feather   step   hinge

Differences in the stone's composition can cause undesirable breaks. At other times, people cause them and won't admit it.

But with lots of practice, people can develop a good understanding of the cone principle, and create very intricate tools.

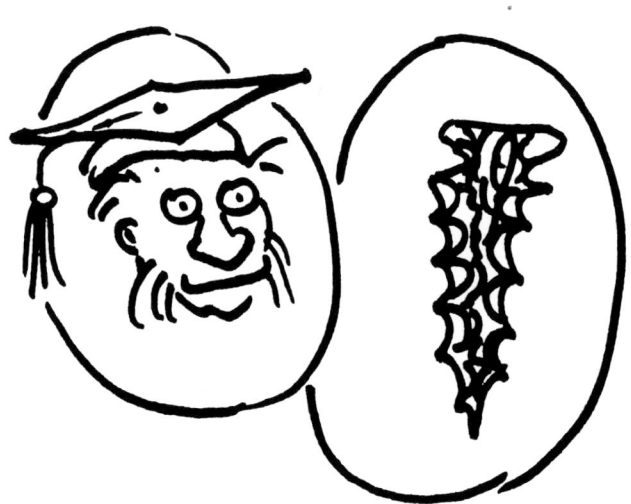

Flintknapper's Tool Kit

A tool kit includes all the manufacturing implements necessary to make flaked tools. This includes percussors, pressure tools, abraders, and leather pads.

Tools are used for three general methods of flaking.

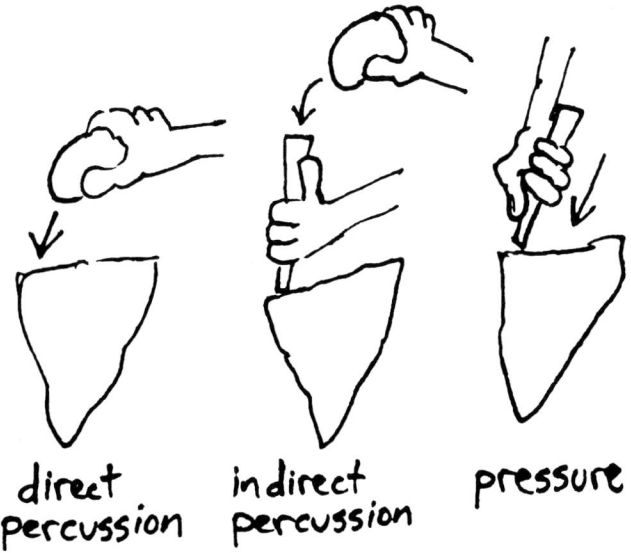

direct percussion   indirect percussion   pressure

<u>Direct percussion</u> is simply striking the stone with a hammer or <u>percussor</u>. Percussors include hammerstones and billets.

Round sandstone and limestone serve as hammerstones, while softer material such as antler, horn, or wood serve as <u>billets</u>. Swung like a hammer, a billet creates a longer and wider flake. Moose antler is preferred because of its density.

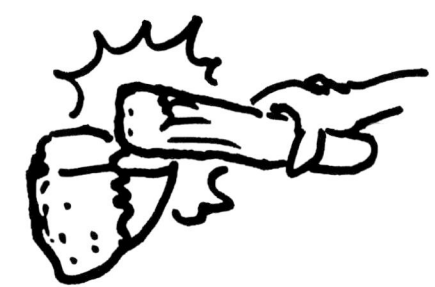

<u>Pressure flaking</u> does not involve hammering. Instead, a pointed tool is used to push the flakes off. Antler and copper work well because they grip the stone without slipping. Pressure tools are highly specialized.

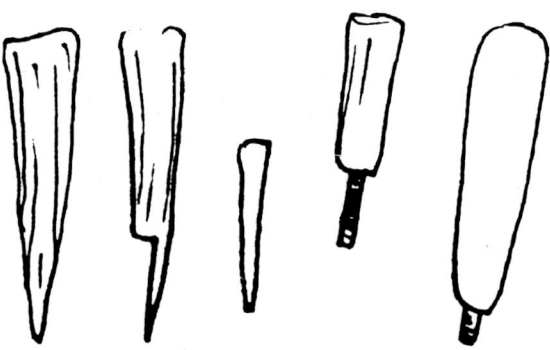

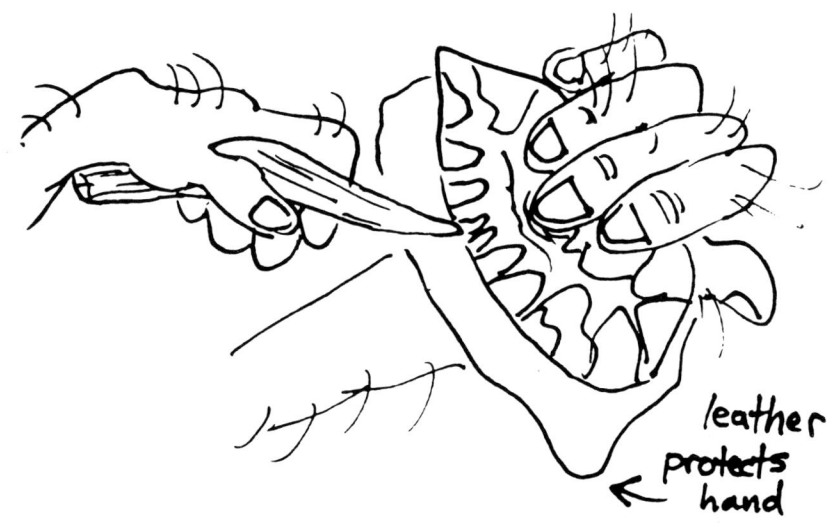

leather protects hand

Pressure flaking is usually done to finalize a product. Very small projectile points such as arrowheads can be made with this method.

An alternate pressure tool is a <u>chest crutch </u>or <u>shoulder crutch</u>--it utilizes a person's body weight to direct all force to a single place on the stone. Don Crabtree used a chest crutch to replicate microblades.

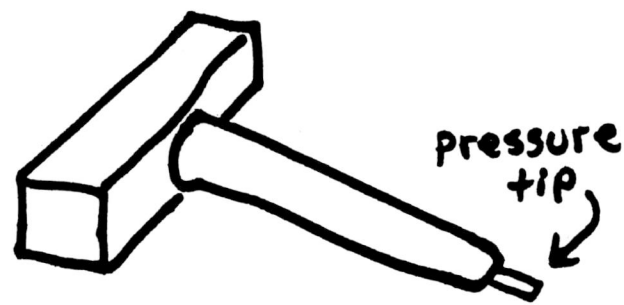

pressure tip

Indirect percussion is somewhat a combination of pressure and direct percussion. A <u>punch</u> is held securely against the stone and is tapped by a hammerstone.

Like those of today's craftsmen, tool kits of the early hunters and gatherers varied from person to person. Each person had a preference of which tool to use for a certain job.

Today, some say it's cheating to make knapping easier with modern tools. <u>Folk-knapping</u> refers to the modern method of producing artifacts with tools that were unavailable to early man.

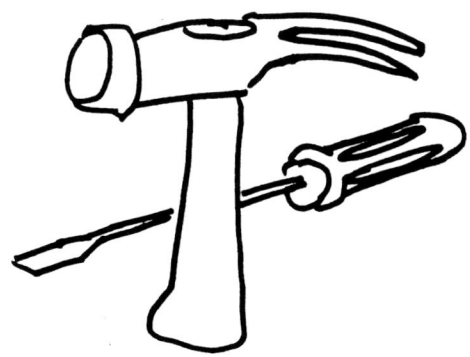

Safety gear should be included in modern knappers' tool kits. Chips of glass are slammed around every time a flake is struck. The razor sharp granules are very DANGEROUS!

safety glasses

gloves

hand pad

leg pad

Before safety glasses, there must have been a lot of one-eyed flintknappers.

Without the use of leather gloves, bloody
fingers are unavoidable.

Manufacturing Stages

Flintknapping is a <u>reduction</u> process. Materials are broken down into smaller, finished products. Less work is expended by starting with a rock similar to the shape and size of the intended stone tool.

Many different kinds of tools are made with flintknapping technology.

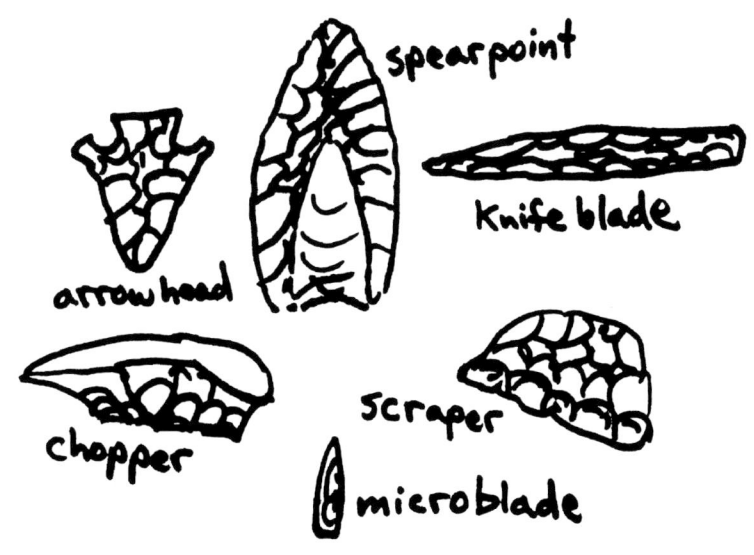

spearpoint

knife blade

arrowhead

chopper

scraper

microblade

Researchers agree a flintknapper uses a series
of stages when making a tool. The actual
number of stages is debatable, but the idea is
basically breaking down material in steps to
maximize efficiency and minimize waste.

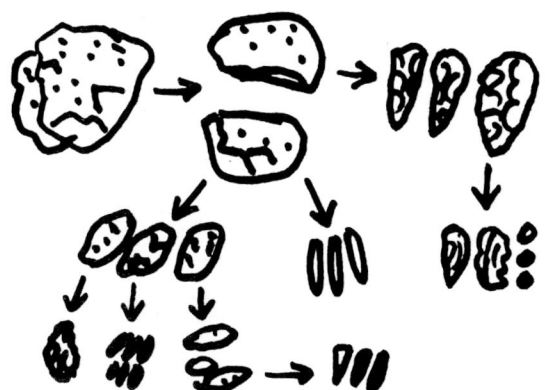

A large cobble is reduced to blanks and cores. A <u>blank</u> is a piece of stone intended for further modification and may yield many different kinds of tools. <u>Cores</u> are specifically intended for blade production.

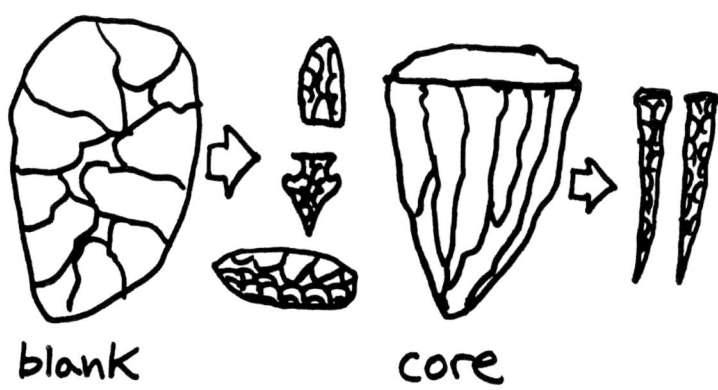

blank   core

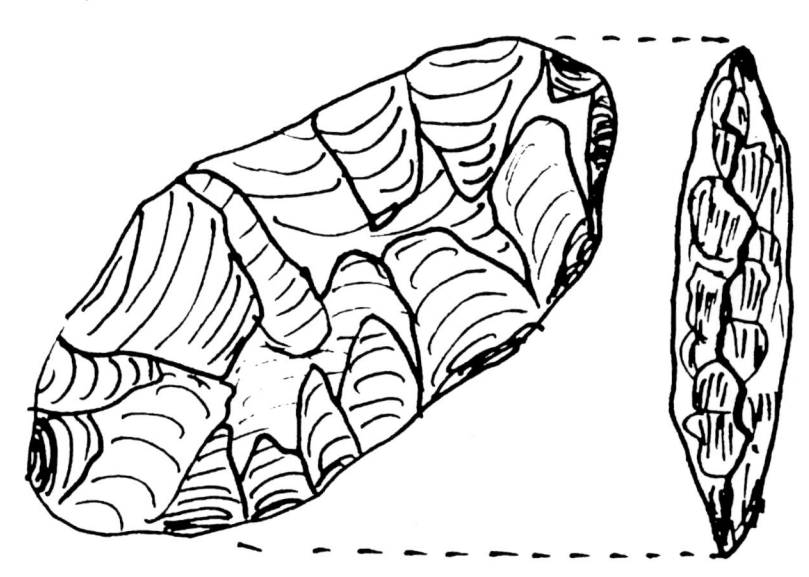

Blanks that are flaked on both sides are called <u>bifaces</u>.

Blanks are further modified into <u>preforms</u>. A preform resembles the shape of a specific tool. By analyzing a preform, you can guess what kind of tool was being made. Technically, a blank could be a preform of a larger tool.

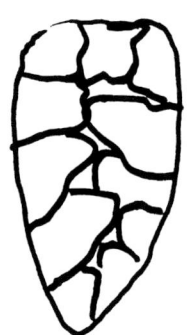

Quarries and Mining

The phrase "cutting edge of technology" probably developed during prehistoric times. People went through great efforts to find the best stone with the sharpest edges.

The sedimentary flint beds of Alibates, Texas, show that people would dig tens of meters to recover less brittle, unweathered flint. Whether it be underground or above ground, anywhere that man gathers stone from the earth is called a <u>quarry</u>. At these sites, rocks and cobbles are examined for quality before being carried away.

Certain indicators will determine if the stone is good enough to use.

After looking at it and tapping it, the flintknapper hammers off a test flake. How the material flakes ultimately determines its worthiness. Quarries may have been the earliest places for hunters to shop.

As large rocks are broken into transportable cobbles, they are carried away to nearby locations called <u>workshops</u>. The workshops are the places where tools begin to take shape with the process of flaking. Each quarry may have hundreds of workshops.

Workshops may have provided places to work safely and privately.

Or maybe people were just looking out for their neighbors.

Whatever the reason, hundreds of flakes were left at the workshops instead of the quarries. People gathered enough good material at the quarry to keep them busy for awhile at the workshops.

Knappers remove all the <u>cortex</u>, or outer covering, and produce blanks and cores for easy transport. Everything carried away from the workshops will be later reduced to tools.

Artifacts found at workshops include: <u>debitage</u> or waste flakes; <u>microdebitage</u> or microscopic flakes; manufacturing tools such as hammerstones and scrapers; and worn-out, end-of-the-line tools. These abandoned artifacts give clues to how early people made stone tools.

Junked tools are sometimes called
<u>rejectamenta</u>. Since many of these tools are
made of stone from a different area, it is
believed that people traveled to quarries and
replaced their tool kits with better stone.

Blanks, made at the workshops, could have been used as trade items for early people. Archaeologists have found caches that are quite far from the stone's source. Workable stone must have been highly valued.

Tool Production and Techniques

It takes experience and practice to become a skilled flintknapper. An expert can make it look easy, but beginners should not try impressing people too early.

Advanced flintknapping techniques relied on knowledge learned from previous generations. Over time, many techniques were developed.

One way to split a large cobble in half is called the <u>bipolar</u> method. The stone is set on an anvil and struck in the middle.

One of the first steps for toolmaking is removing all the <u>cortex.</u> This is the rough, weathered outer layer.

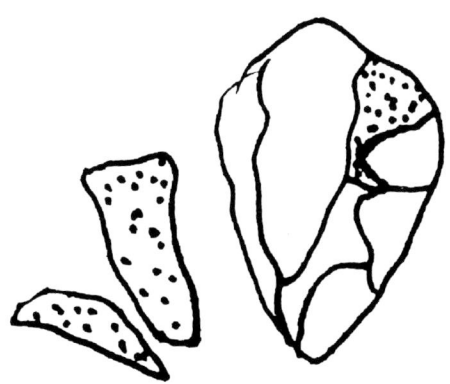

Failure to remove all cortex may cause manufacturing problems later.

Marginal grinding is one of the keys to successful flaking. An abrader stone is used to grind the margins in order to create a flat and sturdy platform. Grinding helps prevent crushing the edges when applying force.

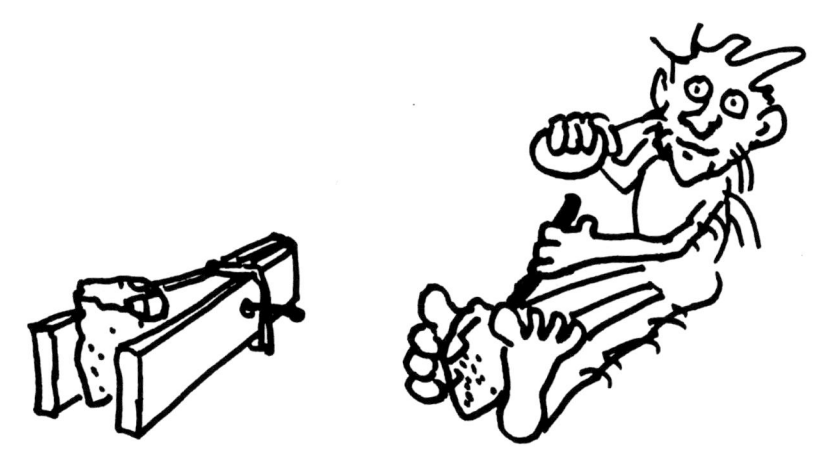

Indirect percussion is good for precision
flaking. A punch can be held at a precise
angle and location on the platform. The stone
can be held by a vise or your feet...

...or another person.

Clay can also be used to support a piece of stone while it is flaked.

Some kinds of stone are more workable after <u>heat treatment</u>. This is really important for various flints. Preforms are placed in a pit between layers of sand and hot coals. The stone is "baked" for 24 hours or until the coals burn out. Flint may change from gray to pink or other colors with a waxy luster. The heat alters the chemical structure of the stone, making it more glassy and easier to flake.

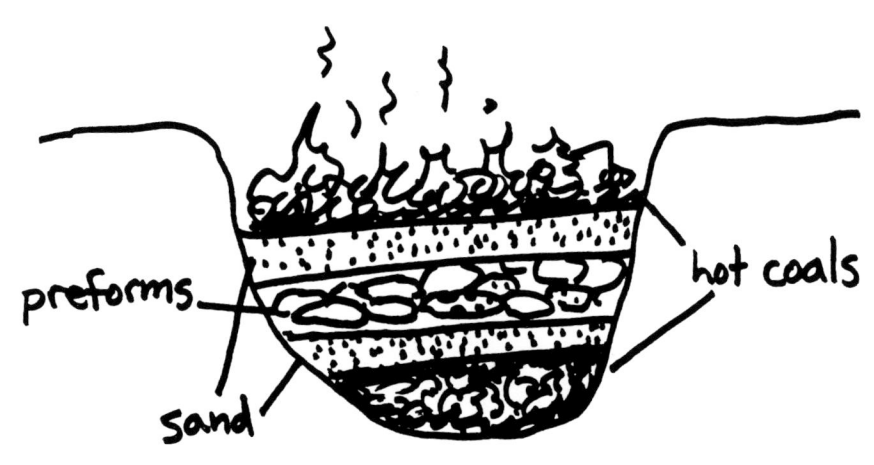

preforms

sand

hot coals

Early hunters made projectile points so they could be <u>hafted</u>, or connected to wooden shafts. This usually involved notching the stone points so they could be tied to a shaft with animal sinew.

<u>Fluting</u> is a technology developed for better hafting. Fluted points have long, longitudinal flake scars usually on both sides. These channels allow the point to fit snugly into the end of a notched shaft.

Fluted points were used over 10,000 years
ago to kill large animals such as mammoths
and bison.

The method in detaching a flute is difficult.
Techniques involve pressure, indirect
percussion, or mechanical lever devices.

The <u>atlatl dart point</u> was a later variation of the hafted spearpoint. It was designed to break away from the main shaft after striking its target. Hunters were assured that the spearpoint would remain in the animal, while the shaft could be recovered without damage.

A widely used technology since the Upper Paleolithic Era was blade production. The idea is to detach similar flakes one after another from a central <u>core</u>. The long, narrow flakes are called <u>blades</u>.

cores   blades

The goal of blade making is to produce as much cutting edge as possible without wasting stone.

A <u>primary core</u> is the first chunk of material that yields flakes. A <u>secondary core</u> can be removed from a primary core and has the same purpose of providing flakes. Flakes are called <u>flake-blanks</u> if they are intended for further modification.

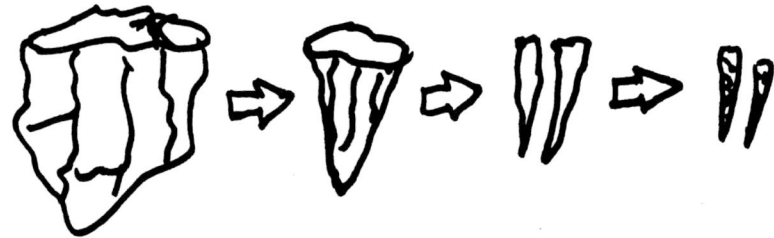

The more blades you can make from a core, the more cutting edge you have. This is why good technique is important.

The hardest part of blade technology is preparing a core. It's important to remember that a successful flake depends on a vertical ridge. To detach a flake, you strike on the ridge of the previous flake scar. Blades are removed until the core is too small.

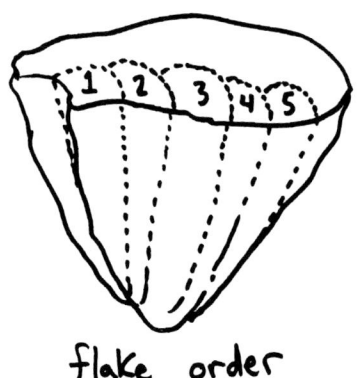

flake order

Sometimes alternate flaking must be used to form a vertical ridge on a core. The first blade removed along this ridge is called a <u>crested blade</u>.

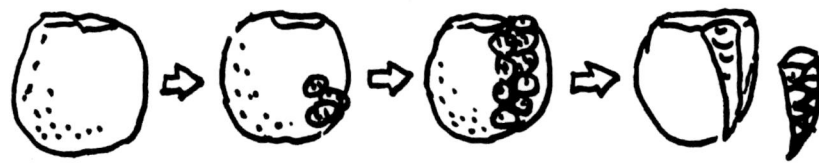

The distal end of the core should be secured against something firm or the blade will curl off towards the base when struck. Direct percussion, indirect percussion, or pressure can be used.

<u>Polyhedral cores</u> of Central America have a distinct shape and look like miniature cucumbers after all the blades are removed. The blades made from these cylindrical cores are called <u>prismatic blades</u>.

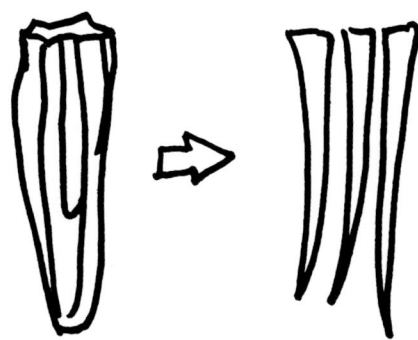

Microblades, which are less than a couple inches long, are generally made with pressure. The first microblade cores were conical or wedge-shaped. The Dyuktai technique of Siberia is one of the oldest microblade technologies. One step was creating a platform by removing a flake off the top. This flake is called a ski spall.

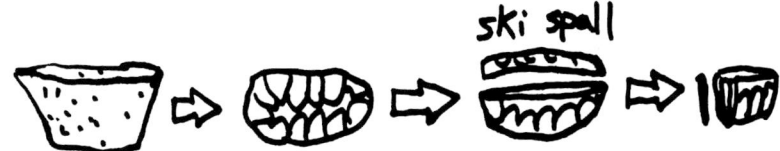

ski spall

Some tools were more efficient with an obtuse edge. Early hunters used obtuse-edged scrapers to clean the flesh off animals skins for making leather and fur garmets. They also used chisel-like tools called <u>burins</u>, to carve antler or wood. Burins may be either obtuse or acute, but an obtuse edge may last longer and may work just as well.

Approaches to Toolmaking

Depending on a task, tools were either 1) made as they were needed, or 2) made for a later use.

<u>Expedient tools</u> were made as they were needed and then discarded at the same place. They were made quickly and with less care. Expedient tools provided a simple solution to an immediate job.

Formal tools were made before they were actually needed. Time and care was spent to make a tool that functioned well and could be used more than once. While a formal tool is easily linked to a specific purpose, it's difficult to tell exactly what an expedient tool was used for.

THIS IS DEFINITELY A SPEAR POINT. BUT WHAT THE HECK DO YOU SUPPOSE THIS ONE WAS USED FOR?

The idea of <u>curation</u> is closely related to formal tools. Curated tools were kept and carried around with anticipation that sometime they would be needed. The materials for these tools were found while doing other things like hunting, trading, and gathering. Tool preparedness was <u>embedded</u> in everyday activities. The goal was to be efficient in terms of finding, manufacturing, and using the stone.

Formal tools can be categorized as being 1) reliable or 2) maintainable. <u>Reliable tools</u> were specially crafted with stronger parts and were used sparingly to prolong tool life. <u>Maintainable tools</u> were light and portable, and were easily repaired during use.

Typology and Function

Whenever mammoth bones are discovered, the question is "Are tools present that indicate butchering?"

Stone tools represent specific activities in history. The mammoth may have been hunted or scavenged.

At first, researchers and collectors were only interested in the shape and description of artifacts. But by studying the function of stone tools, we can learn a lot about the way prehistoric people lived.

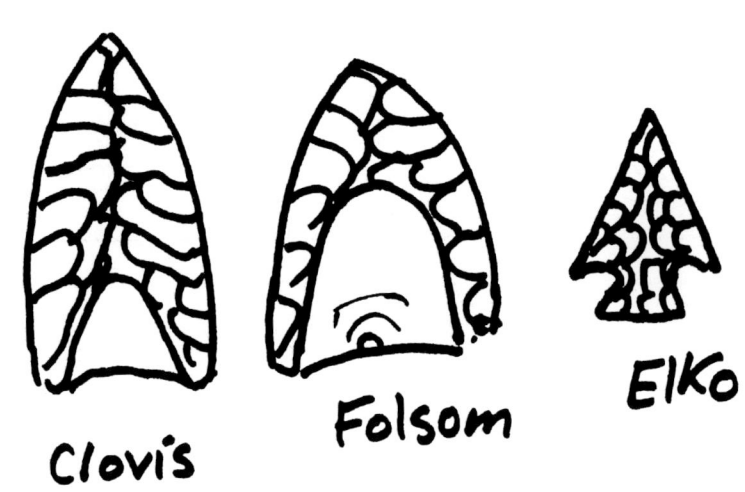

Clovis

Folsom

Elko

Artifacts can be classified by shape, size, and other attributes. This is known as <u>typology</u>.

Whether or not specific types can be matched to specific time periods remains a debated issue. Those who support typology as a valid time marker argue that toolmakers of certain eras favored specific characteristics and consistently produced similar tools. Typology may show the progression from simple to advanced technology over time.

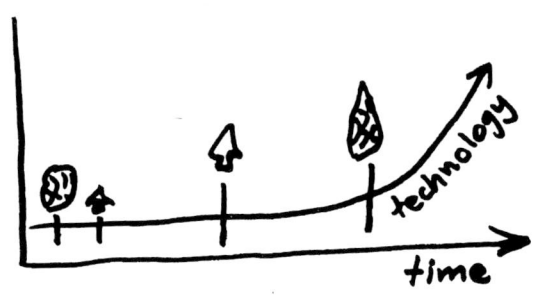

Some types are classified according to where the notch is.

corner   side   unshouldered

The other argument is that typology cannot serve as a valid time marker. This is based on the assumption that when a tool breaks, it goes through a process of <u>rejuvenation</u>. The tool is broken and repaired until it is no longer useful. A discarded tool may look completely different from its original shape.

Because of the possibility of rejuvenation, it's impossible to determine the stages a stone went through by just looking at the end product. However, by studying characteristics of debitage flakes, such as cone scars, a knowledgeable person may be able to link the transition from one shape to another.

<u>Replication</u> involves duplicating the entire process of making a stone tool. This includes using the same material, the same reduction technology, and the same intent in producing a specific tool. Replication provides firsthand knowledge of how tools were made.

However, it's argued that some researchers have gone too far in trying to relive the Stone Age through replication experiments. This is sometimes called <u>macho rocksmanship</u>.

Final Note

Predictable breaking patterns allowed man to manufacture handy tools. Without the kind of stone that exhibits the cone principle, humanity may not be what it is today.

TODAY'S HEADLINES

SPACE SHUTTLE REPAIRS SATELLITE

WHAT IT COULD HAVE BEEN

NEARING 21ST CENTURY AND STILL NO GLASSY ROCKS.

Flintknapping is more difficult than it looks and takes lots of practice to master. Early hunters were highly skilled craftsmen and deserve the same respect as today's skilled craftsmen.

More Information

Canyon Publishing Company, Canoga Park, California

Flintknapping: The Art of Making Stone Tools by Paul Hellweg, 1984.

Idaho Museum of Natural History, Pocatello, Idaho

An Introduction to Flintworking, Occasional Paper #28 by Don E. Crabtree, 1972.

Experiments in Flintworking, Special Publication #2 by Don E. Crabtree, 1971.

Experiments in Flintworking Vol. II, Special Publication #10 by Don E. Crabtree and John D. Speth, 1985.

University of Idaho, Moscow, Idaho

"Anthropology 449: Lithic Technology," classroom lecture instructed by Lee Sappington.

Index